# 200 juices & smoothies

# 200 juices & smoothies

hamlyn **all color**

An Hachette UK Company
www.hachette.co.uk

First published in Great Britain in 2008 by Hamlyn,
a division of Octopus Publishing Group Ltd
2–4 Heron Quays, London E14 4JP
www.octopusbooksusa.com

Copyright © Octopus Publishing Group Ltd 2010

Distributed in the U.S. and Canada by Octopus Books USA:
c/o Hachette Book Group
237 Park Avenue
New York NY 10017

The recipes in this book have previously appeared in other
books published by Hamlyn.

ISBN: 978-0-600-62091-4

Printed and bound in China

1 2 3 4 5 6 7 8 9 10

Standard level spoon measurements are used in all recipes.

¾ cup makes 1 average serving.
All fruit and vegetables should be washed before use.
Fresh herbs should be used unless otherwise stated.
All yogurt should be live unless otherwise stated.

This book includes dishes made with nuts and nut derivatives.
It is advisable for those with known allergic reactions to nuts
and nut derivatives and those who may be potentially
vulnerable to these allergies, such as pregnant and nursing
mothers, invalids, the elderly, babies, and children, to avoid
dishes made with nuts and nut oils. It is also prudent to check
the labels of pre-prepared ingredients for the possible inclusion
of nut derivatives.

# contents

# introduction

# juicing is the answer

These days it is impossible to escape the fact that we need to eat at least five portions of fruit and vegetables every day to make sure that we enjoy good health throughout our lives. Today's busy lifestyles mean that more often than not we find ourselves grabbing food as and when we can, giving little thought to its nutritional content and more to convenience and speed of preparation.

All research points to the fact, however, that both our long-term and short-term wellbeing depends on our being more careful about what we eat, especially when it comes

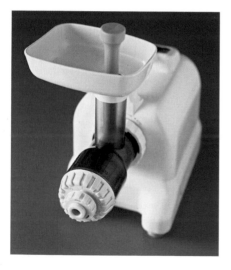

## five good reasons to juice

• Juicing will help our bodies recover from illness and protect us against disease.

• Juicing can make sure that we get our daily recommended intake of vitamins and minerals easily.

• The folic acid found in fruit and vegetables contributes to both healthy hair and nails.

• The antioxidants in fruit and vegetables are essential for healthy, attractive skin.

• Juicing is a convenient and healthful way of supporting a weight-loss program.

to fruit and vegetables. We should learn to regard food as an important and valuable commodity that will not only enable our bodies to perform at their optimum best for as long as possible but also improve our appearance.

## nutritional benefits

Fruit and vegetables are cheap and easily available, and supermarkets and many smaller stores now offer a far wider range than ever before. Even though juicing requires practically no preparation and very little clearing up, many of us still find ourselves opting for a bag of chips or a cookie, rather than a fresh juice. Not only is there no nutritional value in junk food, but we will need to eat it more often and in greater quantities in order to feel satisfied.

It's perfectly understandable that most of us will find the idea of eating our way through a bag of apples or a pile of green vegetables every day hard work, and this is why juicing is such an attractive alternative: juices are quick and easy to prepare, they are delicious to drink, and they are satisfying and nourishing. Combining several different fruits and vegetables in your regular juices is one of the easiest ways of helping you achieve your quota of at least five a day in no time at all.

## why juice at home?

So what is the difference between making your own juice and buying a carton? The most obvious difference is that the nutrients present in fresh, homemade juice far surpass anything you can buy. This is because bought juice has been presqueezed, packaged, and usually diluted with water, so that many of the nutrients are lost along the way. There may also be additives in bought juices, including preservatives, whereas at home you can be sure of exactly what you are drinking.

Not only does homemade juice taste better, but the nutrients can be rapidly assimilated into the body. This can, in fact, be a bit of a shock to your body because it is a detoxification process that can cause a slight headache. When you begin to drink your own juices you might also find that you are passing water more often. However, once your body has adjusted to your new regime, the symptoms will fade and you will feel—and look—great.

# making the best juices and smoothies

If you are a newcomer to juices and smoothies it is best not to rush out and buy a lot of expensive equipment. Smoothies can easily be made in a food processor or blender. However, if you are planning to make juices regularly you will find it is worth investing in a good machine.

## which juicer?

There are several models of juicer on the market these days, and your choice will probably depend as much on how much you want to spend as to how effective the juicer will be. There are two basic options: a masticating juicer, which forces ingredients through a wire mesh, thereby extracting as much juice as possible as it does so, and a centrifugal juicer, which uses spinning blades to separate the pulp from the juice. The centrifugal juicer produces less juice, but it is a cheaper option for beginners.

## let's juice

**1** Assemble your ingredients, but don't prepare them until the last minute to avoid discoloration.
**2** Wash or scrub ingredients that you are keeping whole—such as carrots or parsnips—and peel them only if absolutely necessary.

**3** Roughly chop and measure the ingredients according to the recipe.

## what is a smoothie?

Unlike a juice, a smoothie is made in a food processor or blender. It is thicker than a juice, and most include extra ingredients such as yogurt, honey, ice cream, or milk as well as fruit and juices. A smoothie is even quicker and easier to make than juice because all the ingredients go straight into the machine and are simply processed for a few seconds.

One of the best ways of making a really good smoothie is to use frozen fruits. The process of freezing means that the vitamins and nutrients are retained in the fruits, and frozen produce allows you to enjoy seasonal fruits and vegetables all year round. Your drink will be naturally chilled and won't need to be diluted with ice or chilled water.

## juices & smoothies for kids

Making sure that your children get a minimum of five fruits and vegetables a day can be a battle, but juices and smoothies are a great way to make sure they get all the nutrients needed for a healthy, growing body. Most kids love them, and your life will be easier if you don't have to try and get them to eat broccoli.

# choosing the best ingredients

There are very few fruit or vegetables that can't be used in juices and smoothies, and although the idea of eating portions of parsnips and pineapple together might not fill you with enthusiasm this combination works surprisingly well as a juice. However, there are a few firm favorites that appear time and time again, and following is a round-up of some of the best fruit and vegetables.

Buy organic fruit and vegetables whenever possible to avoid residual pesticides and wash or scrub them thoroughly before use to remove dirt and germs.

## apples

Not only are apples full of antioxidants, but they have a naturally sweet flavor that complements sour and savory ingredients really well. Use apples unpeeled or juice them whole, including the seeds, to gain the maximum nutritional benefit—the antioxidant quercetin, for example, is found only in the skin. The fresher the apple the more vitamin C it will contain.

## oranges and other citrus fruits

These are one of the best sources of vitamin C, and also one of the most popular mixers in juices and smoothies. Some recipes suggest that you remove the skin but leave some of the pith attached to the segments to increase the vitamin content of your drinks.

## bananas

Bananas are especially useful in smoothies because they help to create a thick, smooth, tasty drink. Bananas can be peeled, sliced, and frozen overnight to make a cool drink the next day. They are full of carbohydrates and an ideal energy booster or quick snack.

## strawberries

Both beneficial and delicious, strawberries are a good source of vitamin C, calcium, and potassium. To make the most of this universal favorite freeze the fruits when in season and add them to smoothies all year round.

## pears

Pears are delicious in juices. Not only do they combine well with other fruits and vegetables, but they are also ideal for children because they rarely cause an allergic reaction. They are full of vitamin C, potassium, and beta-carotene and a quick source of energy.

## peaches

This fruit can be a boon if you suffer from stomach upsets because of its antioxidant qualities. It is also a good source of vitamin C.

## apricots

Both fresh and dried apricots can be used in juices and smoothies. Dried apricots tend to be much sweeter than the fresh fruit but they have a high beta-carotene and potassium content.

## cranberries

If you suffer from urinary infections cranberry juice could be the answer. The fruits are rich in vitamin C and potassium, and they are delicious in juices, adding a bittersweet flavor and vibrant color.

## blackberries

Rich in vitamin C and full of antioxidants, blackberries are good for building a healthy immune system. The fresh fruit freezes well and can be added to smoothies all year round.

## mangoes

A mango will add an exotic flavor to drinks, and the fruit also contains a high level of vitamin C, fiber, and potassium. It is a great fruit to keep on your shopping list.

## watermelons

Yielding large amounts of juice, watermelons are a great antioxidant, detoxing, and diuretic fruit. They are also a firm favorite with children because of their mild, sweet flavor.

## avocados

Avocados are full of protein and are filling and nutritious. They are rich in vitamin E, which is beneficial to the skin and helps maintain healthy circulation. Eat avocados as soon as they are ripe as they start to lose important antioxidants as they ripen. Cut them and remove the skin and pits at the very last minute to avoid discoloration.

## tomatoes

It is believed that tomatoes may help lower the risk of certain cancers, and this is attributed to the lycopene they contain. They are also high in vitamin C and fiber. Adding tomatoes to savory juices boosts their nutrient content and makes them colorful.

## carrots

Carrots are great energy food and are an aid to good digestion because of their fiber content; they are also full of beta-carotene and alpha-carotene, and are delicious in both fruit and vegetable juices.

## spinach

Some people recoil at the idea of spinach in a drink, but, as the saying goes, don't knock it until you've tried it. Rich in iron and beta-carotene, spinach is great for vegetarians.

## beet

Beet is a great source of folic acid and fiber. Surprisingly perhaps, it is delicious when combined with citrus fruits, making a tangy and colorful juice.

## celery

Celery is a great cleanser and is rich in phyto-nutrients. A few sticks of celery produce a good yield of juice, and it is much more easily digested as juice than in its raw state.

## ginger

Renowned in many traditional diets as an immunity booster, ginger helps to fight bugs with its high levels of zinc. It is also said to be settling for the stomach and is particularly useful for mothers-to-be who are suffering from morning sickness.

## live yogurt

Live yogurt is a valuable source of calcium and vitamin D. It helps to maintain good health, because it contains cultures with health-giving properties. Including yogurt in a smoothie is a good way of giving a child who doesn't like milk a calcium boost.

## soy

Soy is rich in protein and calcium. It makes an excellent alternative to dairy products for those who are lactose-intolerant, and it helps to lower cholesterol levels. It is also useful for controlling the symptoms of the menopause.

# fruit juices

# watermelon & strawberry juice

Makes ¾ **cup**

1 ⅓ cups **strawberries**, plus
   extra to serve (optional)
7 oz **watermelon**
**small handful of mint leaves**,
   plus sprigs to decorate
2–3 **ice cubes**

**Hull** the strawberries. Skin and seed the melon and cut
the flesh into cubes.

**Transfer** the fruit to a food processor or blender, add the
mint, and process with a couple of ice cubes.

**Pour** into a glass, decorate with mint sprigs and whole or
sliced strawberries, if desired, and serve immediately.

**For watermelon & cranberry juice**, simply replace the
strawberries with 1 ¼ cups cranberries and add 7 oz
cucumber. This makes a longer, more refreshing, and
slightly tangy drink.

# watermelon & raspberry juice

Makes 1½ **cups**

about 10 oz **watermelon**
1 cup **raspberries**
2–3 **ice cubes**

**Skin** and seed the melon and cut the flesh into cubes.
Juice the melon with the raspberries.

**Pour** into a glass, add a couple of ice cubes, and serve
immediately.

**For watermelon & orange juice**, juice 2 oranges instead
of the raspberries.

# papaya, raspberry, & grapefruit juice

Makes ¾ **cup**

5 oz **papaya**
5 oz **grapefruit**
1¼ cups **raspberries**
juice of ½ **lime**, plus slices
   to serve (optional)
2–3 **ice cubes** (optional)

**Scoop** out the flesh of the papaya. Segment the grapefruit, leaving the pith on, and juice it with the papaya and raspberries and lime juice.

**Pour** into a glass, add the ice cubes, if using, and decorate with lime slices if desired.

**For papaya & orange juice**, replace the grapefruit and raspberries with the juice of 2 oranges and 4 oz cucumber.

# pineapple, grape, & celery juice

Makes ¾ **cup**

4 oz **pineapple**
¾ cup seedless **green grapes**
1 large **celery stick**
2 oz **lettuce**, plus extra to
   serve (optional)
2–3 **ice cubes** (optional)

**Remove** the skin and core from the pineapple and roughly chop the flesh. Juice the pineapple with the grapes, celery, and lettuce.

**Pour** the juice into a glass over ice, if using, decorate with pieces of lettuce, if desired, and serve immediately.

**For pineapple & pear juice**, double the amount of pineapple and replace the grapes, celery, and lettuce with 2 pears and half a lime. This juice is rich in vitamins as well as being delicious.

# celery, ginger, & pineapple juice

Makes ¾ **cup**

3 **celery sticks**
4 oz **pineapple**
1 inch piece **fresh ginger root**
**crushed ice**

**Trim** the celery and cut it into 2 inch lengths. Remove the peel and core from the pineapple and chop it into cubes. Peel and roughly chop the ginger. Juice the celery with the pineapple and ginger.

**Transfer** the juice to a food processor or blender and process with a little crushed ice. Pour into a glass and serve immediately.

**For pineapple & pink grapefruit juice**, omit the celery and ginger, double the amount of pineapple, and juice it with the flesh and skin of a pink grapefruit. Top up with still water.

# pineapple & alfalfa juice

Makes **1 cup**

5 oz **pineapple**
5 cups **alfalfa sprouts**, plus
   extra to decorate
2–3 **ice cubes**
3 tablespoons **still water**

**Peel** and core the pineapple, chop the flesh into cubes, and juice.

**Transfer** the pineapple juice to a food processor or blender, add the alfalfa sprouts, ice cubes, and still water and process briefly.

**Pour** the juice into a glass, sprinkle with extra alfalfa sprouts, and serve immediately.

**For pineapple & lettuce juice**, juice 4 oz pineapple with double the amount of lettuce. If you prefer a really slushy drink, blend the resulting juice with some ice cubes.

# blackberry, cantaloupe melon, & kiwifruit juice

Makes **1 cup**

4 oz **cantaloupe melon**
2 **kiwifruit**
¾ cup fresh or frozen
   **blackberries**, plus extra
   to decorate (optional)
2–3 **ice cubes**

**Peel** the melon and cut the flesh into cubes. Leaving on the skins, evenly slice the kiwifruit. Juice the melon and kiwifruit with the blackberries.

**Transfer** the juice to a food processor or blender and process with a couple of ice cubes. Pour into a glass and decorate with a few blackberries, if desired.

**For melon & cherry juice**, skin and roughly chop 10 oz honeydew melon. Juice the melon flesh with ½ cup pitted cherries.

# blackberry, apple, & celeriac juice

Makes ¾ **cup**

4 oz **celeriac**
2 oz **apple**
¾ cup frozen **blackberries**,
    plus extra to decorate
2–3 **ice cubes**

**Peel** the celeriac and cut the flesh into cubes. Roughly chop the apple and juice it with the celeriac.

**Transfer** the juice to a food processor or blender, add the blackberries and a couple of ice cubes, and process briefly.

**Pour** the juice into a glass, decorate with extra blackberries, and serve immediately.

**For blackberry & pineapple juice**, juice 1 cup blackberries and 5 oz pineapple with 1 oz apple. Serve in a tall glass over ice.

# blueberry, apple, & ginger juice

Makes ¾ **cup**

1 inch piece **fresh ginger
  root**, roughly chopped, plus
  extra to serve (optional)
2 cups **blueberries**
4 oz **grapefruit**
8 oz **apples**
**ice cubes** (optional)

**Peel** and roughly chop the ginger. Juice the blueberries, grapefruit, and apple with the ginger.

**Pour** the juice into a glass over ice, if using, decorate with thin slices of ginger, if desired, and serve immediately.

**For apple & ginger juice**, juice 8 oz apple with 1 inch ginger root. If you desire, top it up with ice-cold water.

# summer strawberry juice

Makes ¾ **cup**

¾ cup **strawberries**
7 oz **tomatoes**
**basil leaves**
**ice cubes**

**Hull** the strawberries. Juice the tomatoes with the strawberries and a few basil leaves, reserving 1 basil leaf for decoration.

**Pour** the juice into a glass over ice, decorate with the reserved basil leaf, and serve immediately.

**For strawberry & kiwifruit juice**, wash and hull 1 cup strawberries and juice them with 2 peeled kiwifruit.

# apple, cranberry, & blueberry juice

Makes 1¼ **cups**

3 **apples**
⅔ cup unsweetened **cranberry juice**
1 cup fresh or frozen **blueberries**
1 tablespoon **powdered psyllium husks** (optional)
**ice cubes** (optional)

**Juice** the apples. Transfer the apple juice to a food processor or blender, add the cranberry juice, blueberries, and powdered psyllium husks, if using, and process.

**Pour** the juice into a glass over ice, if using, and serve immediately.

**For cranberry, apple, & lettuce juice**, juice half an apple and 4 oz lettuce with ½ cup cranberries. Serve over ice.

# pear & cranberry juice

Makes ¾ **cup**

1 large **pear**
6 tablespoons **cranberry juice**
**ice cubes**

**Juice** the pear. Mix the pear juice with the cranberry juice.

**Pour** the combined juices into a glass over ice and serve immediately.

**For cranberry & cucumber juice**, use the same amount of cranberry juice and add the juice of 1 orange and 2 oz cucumber.

# orange & raspberry juice

Makes **2 cups**

2 large **oranges**
1½ cups **raspberries**
1 cup **still water**
**ice cubes** (optional)

**Peel** the oranges and divide the flesh into segments.
Juice the orange segments with the raspberries then add
the still water.

**Pour** the juice into 2 tall glasses over ice, if using, and
serve immediately.

**For orange & apricot juice**, juice 10 oz fresh apricots with
1 large orange. Top up with water to taste.

# apple, mango, & passion fruit juice

Makes 1¼ **cups**

1 **mango**
2 **passion fruit**
3 **apples**, preferably red, plus
  extra to serve (optional)
**ice cubes**

**Peel** the mango and remove the pit. Slice the passion fruit in half, scoop out the flesh, and discard the seeds. Juice the apples with the mango and passion fruit.

**Pour** the juice into a tall glass over ice, decorate with apple slices, if desired, and serve immediately.

**For mango & pineapple juice**, juice a peeled and pitted mango with 4 oz pineapple and 3 apples. Top up with ice-cold water, if desired.

# apple, apricot, & peach juice

**Makes ¾ cup**

3 **apricots**
1 **peach**, plus extra to serve
  (optional)
2 **apples**
**ice cubes**

**Halve** and pit the apricots and peach. Juice the apples with the apricots and peach.

**Transfer** the juice to a food processor or blender, add a few ice cubes, and process for 10 seconds.

**Pour** the juice into a glass, decorate with peach slices, if desired, and serve immediately.

**For apple & passion fruit juice**, replace the peach with 2 passion fruit. Juice the apricot, apple, and passion fruit and serve over ice.

# pear, kiwifruit, & lime juice

**Makes 1¼ cups**

3 **kiwifruit**, plus extra to serve
   (optional)
2 ripe **pears**
½ **lime**
2–3 **ice cubes** (optional)

**Peel** the kiwifruit. Slice the kiwifruit, pears, and lime into even-size pieces then juice.

**Pour** into a tall glass, add a couple of ice cubes, if using, decorate with slices of kiwifruit, if desired, and serve immediately.

**For grape & kiwifruit juice**, replace the pears and lime juice with 1½ cups seedless green grapes.

# pear, celery, & ginger juice

Makes ¾ **cup**

1 large **celery stick**
1 inch piece **fresh ginger root**
4 oz **pear**
**ice cubes**

**Trim** the celery and cut it into 2 inch lengths. Peel and roughly chop the ginger. Juice the pear with the celery and ginger.

**Pour** the juice into a glass over ice; alternatively, briefly process the juice in a food processor or blender with 2–3 ice cubes.

**For pear & peach juice**, juice 3 pears with 2 peaches to give a thick, nutritious drink.

# pear, grapefruit, & celery juice

Makes ¾ **cup**

3 oz **grapefruit**
4 oz **lettuce**
2 **celery sticks**
2 oz **pear**
**ice cubes** (optional)

**Peel** the grapefruit and divide it into segments. Separate the lettuce into leaves. Trim the celery and cut it into 2 inch lengths. Chop the pear. Juice the grapefruit with the lettuce, celery, and pear.

**Pour** the juice into a glass over ice, if using, and serve immediately.

**For grapefruit & lemon juice**, peel and segment a grapefruit and juice it with 2 inches cucumber and half a lemon. Top up with sparkling mineral water.

# grape & plum juice

**Makes 1¼ cups**

about 10 oz **plums**, plus extra
  to serve (optional)
1 cup seedless **red grapes**
2–3 crushed **ice cubes**

**Remove** the pits from the plums then cut the flesh into even-size pieces. Juice with the grapes.

**Pour** the juice into a tall glass, add a couple of crushed ice cubes, decorate with grapes or slices of plum, if desired, and serve immediately.

**For plum & orange juice**, replace the grapes with 2 oranges. If you desire, top up with sparkling mineral water.

# grapefruit & orange juice

Makes ¾ **cup**

½ **grapefruit**
1 large **orange**
1 **lime**
**ice cubes** or **sparkling**
  **mineral water**

**Peel** all the fruit, leaving a little of the pith on the segments. If you desire, reserve some of the lime rind to decorate.

**Juice** the fruit, then either serve it over ice or, if you want a longer drink, dilute it with an equal amount of sparkling mineral water. Serve the juice decorated with curls of lime rind, if desired.

**For orange & carrot juice**, peel and segment 2 oranges and juice with 4 oz carrots.

# apricot & pineapple juice

Makes 1½ **cups**

⅓ cup ready-to-eat **dried
  apricots**
1½ cups **pineapple juice**
2–3 **ice cubes**

**Roughly** chop the dried apricots and put them into a large
bowl. Pour over the pineapple juice, cover, and allow to
stand overnight in the refrigerator.

**Transfer** the apricots and juice to a food processor or
blender and process until thick and smooth.

**Pour** the juice into a tall glass, add a couple of ice cubes,
and serve immediately.

**For dried apricot & orange juice**, replace the pineapple
juice with the same quantity of orange juice; alternatively
juice 2 oranges with the apricots for a really fresh taste.

# prune, pear, & spinach juice

**Makes ¾ cup**

3 ready-to-eat **prunes**
8 oz **pear**, plus extra to serve
  (optional)
2½ cups **spinach**
**ice cubes** (optional)

**Remove** the pits from the prunes if necessary. Juice the pears and spinach with the prunes.

**Pour** the juice into a glass over ice, if using, decorate with slices of pear, if desired, and serve immediately.

**For pear & avocado juice**, roughly chop 12 oz pears and blend with 3 oz peeled and pitted avocados.

# orange & passion fruit sparkler

Makes ¾ **cup**

1 small **orange**
1 **passion fruit**
½ cup **sparkling mineral
  water**
2–3 **ice cubes**

**Peel**, segment, and juice the orange. Scoop the flesh out of
the passion fruit and press the pulp through a small strainer
to extract the juice.

**Mix** the orange juice with the passion fruit juice and sparkling
water. Pour into a glass over ice and serve immediately.

**For cherry cranberry fizz**, juice ½ cup pitted cherries and
½ cup cranberries and top up with sparkling mineral water.

# peach & ginger juice

Makes ¾ **cup**

2 **peaches**
1 inch piece **fresh ginger
  root**, roughly chopped
**ice cubes**
**sparkling mineral water**
**mint leaves**, to serve

**Halve** the peaches and remove the pits. Peel and roughly chop the ginger. Juice the peach with the ginger.

**Pour** the juice into a tall glass over ice, add a splash of sparkling mineral water and a couple of mint leaves and serve immediately.

**For grapefruit fizz**, juice 10 oz grapefruit with 2 medium cucumbers and half a lemon. Top up with sparkling mineral water and stir in some chopped mint.

# vegetable juices

# broccoli, parsnip, & apple juice

Makes ¾ **cup**

2 oz **parsnip**
2 oz **apple**
5 oz **broccoli**
2–3 **ice cubes**

**Peel** the parsnip and cut the flesh into chunks. Chop the apple and trim the broccoli. Juice the parsnip with the apple and broccoli.

**Transfer** the juice to a food processor or blender and process with the ice cubes to make a creamy juice.

**Pour** into a glass and serve immediately.

**For broccoli, carrot, & beet juice**, trim 8 oz broccoli and juice it with 6 oz carrots and 2 oz beet.

# broccoli, spinach, & tomato juice

Makes ¾ **cup**

3 cups **spinach**
5 oz **broccoli**
2 **tomatoes**
**celery stick**, to serve
   (optional)

**Rinse** the spinach and trim the broccoli. Juice the tomatoes with the green vegetables, adding the broccoli and spinach alternately so that the spinach leaves do not clog the juicer.

**Pour** the juice into a glass, add a stick of celery, if desired, and serve immediately.

**For spinach & carrot juice**, rinse 5 cups spinach and juice the leaves with 8 oz carrots and ½ cup parsley. Stir in a teaspoon of spirulina, the freshwater algae supplement, for extra energy.

# broccoli, spinach, & apple juice

Makes ¾ **cup**

5 oz **broccoli**
3 cups **spinach**
2 **apples**
2–3 **ice cubes**

**Trim** the broccoli and rinse the spinach. Juice the apples with the spinach and broccoli, alternating the spinach leaves with the other ingredients so that the spinach leaves do not clog the machine.

**Transfer** the juice to a food processor or blender, add a couple of ice cubes, and process briefly.

**Pour** into a glass and serve immediately.

**For spinach, apple, & pepper juice**, use 8 oz apples and, instead of broccoli, juice 4 oz yellow bell pepper. Stir in a pinch of ground cinnamon before serving.

# broccoli & kale juice

Makes ¾ **cup**

4 oz **broccoli**
4 oz **kale**
1 large **celery stick**
½ cup **parsley**
7 oz **apple**
**ice cubes**

**Trim** the broccoli and kale. Trim the celery and cut it into 2 inch lengths. Juice the parsley and apple with the broccoli, kale, and celery.

**Pour** the juice into a glass over ice and serve immediately.

**For broccoli, lettuce, & celery juice**, trim 5 oz broccoli and juice it with 4 oz lettuce and 2–3 celery sticks.

# celeriac, alfalfa, & orange juice

Makes ¾ **cup**

1 small **orange**, plus extra
  to serve (optional)
4 oz **celeriac**
3 cups **alfalfa sprouts**

**Peel** the orange and separate it into segments. Peel the
celeriac and cut it into chunks. Rinse the alfalfa sprouts.
Juice the ingredients.

**Pour** the juice into a glass, add slices of orange, if desired,
and serve immediately.

**For celery, alfalfa, & apple juice**, trim 3 celery sticks and
cut them into 2 inch lengths. Juice them with 2 apples
and 1 cup alfalfa sprouts. This juice is delicious served
ice cold.

# tomato, red pepper, & papaya juice

Makes ¾ **cup**

about 4 oz **papaya**
about 4 oz **red bell pepper**
1 large **tomato**
2–3 **ice cubes**

**Peel** and seed the papaya. Core and seed the pepper. Juice the tomato with the papaya and pepper.

**Transfer** the juice to a food processor or blender, add a couple of ice cubes, and process.

**Pour** the juice into a glass and serve immediately.

**For pepper & orange juice**, core and seed 4 oz each of red, yellow, and orange bell peppers and juice the pepper flesh with 1 orange. Serve sprinkled with chopped mint.

# tomato, carrot, & ginger juice

Makes ⅔ **cup**

1 inch cube **fresh ginger root**
2–3 **celery sticks**, plus extra
   to serve (optional)
10 oz **tomatoes**
6 oz **carrot**
1 **garlic clove**
1 inch piece fresh
   **horseradish**
2–3 **ice cubes**

**Peel** and roughly chop the ginger. Trim the celery and cut it into 2 inch lengths. Juice the tomatoes, carrot, garlic, and horseradish with the ginger and celery.

**Transfer** the juice to a food processor or blender, add a couple of ice cubes, and process briefly.

**Pour** the juice into a small glass, garnish with celery slivers, if desired, and serve immediately.

**For carrot & pink grapefruit juice**, peel and segment a pink grapefruit, leaving some pith, and juice with 2 carrots and 2 apples. Serve topped up with mineral water.

# tomato, red pepper, & cabbage juice

Makes ¾ **cup**

6 oz **red bell pepper**
6 oz **tomatoes**
4 oz **white cabbage**
1 tablespoon chopped
 **parsley**
**lime wedge**, to decorate
 (optional)

**Core** and seed the pepper. Juice the tomatoes and cabbage with the pepper.

**Pour** the juice into a tall glass, stir in the parsley, decorate with a lime wedge, if desired, and serve immediately.

**For tomato, red pepper, & celery juice**, trim 4 celery sticks and cut them into 2 inch lengths. Juice the celery with 3 ripe tomatoes and half a red bell pepper. Add a crushed garlic clove and chopped chili, to taste.

# tomato, lemon, & parsley juice

Makes 1¼ **cups**

2 **celery sticks**, plus leaves
   to serve (optional)
4 **tomatoes**
large handful of **parsley**
zest and juice of ½ **lemon**
**ice cubes**

**Trim** the celery sticks and cut them into 2 inch lengths.
Juice the tomatoes and parsley with the celery, lemon juice
and zest.

**Pour** the juice into a tall glass over ice, add the celery
leaves, if using, and serve immediately.

**For tomato & celery juice**, replace the lemon juice and
zest and the parsley with Tabasco sauce, celery salt, and
black pepper, to taste.

# tomato, apple, & basil juice

Makes ¾ **cup**

1 **celery stick**
4 large **tomatoes**
1 **apple**
**ice cubes**
4 **basil leaves,** finely chopped
1½ tablespoons **lime juice**
extra **basil leaves,** to serve
   (optional)

**Trim** the celery and cut it into 2 inch lengths. Juice the tomatoes and apple with the celery.

**Pour** the juice into a glass over ice, stir in the basil leaves and lime juice, shred extra basil leaves and add, if desired, and serve immediately.

**For tomato, cauliflower, & carrot juice**, trim 4 oz cauliflower and juice with 1 large tomato and 7 oz carrot.

# celery & celeriac juice

Makes **1 cup**

2–3 **celery sticks**
5 oz **celeriac**
4 oz **lettuce**
2 cups **spinach**
2–3 **ice cubes**

**Trim** the celery and cut it into 2 inch lengths. Peel the celeriac and cut the flesh into cubes. Separate the lettuce into leaves. Juice the celery, celeriac, lettuce, and spinach, alternating the ingredients so that the lettuce and spinach leaves do not clog the machine.

**Transfer** the juice to a food processor or blender, add a couple of ice cubes, and process briefly.

**Pour** the juice into a tall glass and serve immediately.

**For carrot, celery, & celeriac juice**, peel 4 oz celeriac and trim and cut 4 celery sticks into 2 inch lengths. Juice the celeriac and celery with 1 carrot.

# carrot, beet, & sweet potato juice

Makes ¾ **cup**

6 oz **sweet potato** or **yam**
4 oz **beet**
6 oz **carrot**
4 oz **fennel**
**ice cubes**
**fennel fronds**, to decorate
   (optional)

**Peel** the sweet potato or yam and scrub the beet. Juice the carrot and fennel with the sweet potato and beet.

**Pour** the juice into a glass over ice, decorate with fennel fronds, if desired, and serve immediately.

**For carrot, beet, & orange juice**, replace the sweet potato and fennel with ¾ cup strawberries and 1 orange. This colorful juice will give you an instant energy boost.

# carrot, cabbage, & apple juice

Makes ¾ **cup**

6 oz **carrot**
8 oz **apple**
4 oz **red cabbage**
**orange slices**, to decorate
**ice cubes**

**Roughly** chop the carrot and apple and juice them with the cabbage.

**Pour** the juice into a glass over ice, decorate with a slice of orange, and serve immediately.

**For carrot, spinach, & pink grapefruit juice**, juice 4 oz each of carrot, spinach, and pink grapefruit. This juice has a pleasantly astringent flavor.

# carrot, fennel, & ginger juice

**Makes ¾ cup**

1 inch piece **fresh ginger root**
2 **celery sticks**
10 oz **carrot**
2 oz **fennel**, plus extra to
   serve (optional)
1 tablespoon **spirulina**
   (optional)
**ice cubes** (optional)
**fennel fronds**, to decorate
   (optional)

**Peel** and roughly chop the ginger. Trim the celery and cut
it into 2 inch lengths. Juice the carrot, fennel, and spirulina,
if using, with the ginger and celery.

**Pour** the juice into a glass over ice, if using, decorate with
strips of fennel and fennel fronds, if desired, and serve
immediately.

**For carrot, apple, & ginger juice**, peel and roughly chop
½ inch cube fresh ginger root and juice it with 2 carrots
and 1 tart apple, such as a Granny Smith.

# carrot & lettuce juice

Makes ¾ **cup**

4 oz **carrot**
7 oz **lettuce**
**ice cubes**
chopped **cilantro leaves**,
   to decorate

**Chop** the carrot into chunks and separate the lettuce leaves. Juice the carrot with the lettuce, taking care that the lettuce leaves do not clog the machine.

**Pour** the juice into a glass over ice, decorate with chopped cilantro, and serve immediately.

**For carrot & green leaf juice**, add 2 celery sticks, 2 cups spinach, and ½ cup parsley to the carrot and lettuce.

# carrot & kiwifruit juice

Makes **1 cup**

about 7 oz **carrot**
1 **kiwifruit**, plus extra to serve
  (optional)
**ice cubes** (optional)

**Cut** the carrot and kiwifruit into even-size pieces and juice together.

**Pour** the juice into a glass over ice, if using, decorate with slices of kiwifruit, if desired, and serve immediately.

**For cucumber & kiwifruit juice**, omit the carrots and instead juice 1½ cucumbers with the kiwifruit. Serve with a squeeze of lemon.

# carrot, parsnip, & sweet potato juice

Makes ¾ **cup**

6 oz **celery**
6 oz **carrot**
6 oz **parsnip**
6 oz **sweet potato**
handful of **parsley**, plus extra
  to serve (optional)
1 **garlic clove**
2–3 **ice cubes**
**lemon wedge**

**Trim** the celery and cut it into 2 inch lengths. Juice the carrot, parsnip, sweet potato, parsley, and garlic with the celery.

**Transfer** the juice to a food processor or blender and process with a couple of ice cubes.

**Pour** the juice into a glass, decorate with a wedge of lemon and a parsley sprig, if desired, and serve immediately.

**For carrot, parsnip, & melon juice**, which is especially rich in folic acid, juice 4 oz each of carrot, parsnip, lettuce, and cantaloupe melon.

# carrot, radish, & cucumber juice

Makes ¾ **cup**

4 oz **potato**
4 oz **radish**, plus extra
   to serve (optional)
4 oz **carrot**
4 oz **cucumber**
**ice cubes**

**Juice** the potato, radish, carrot, and cucumber.

**Transfer** the juice to a food processor or blender, add a couple of ice cubes, and process briefly.

**Pour** the juice into a tall glass over ice, decorate with slices of radish, if desired, and serve immediately.

**For carrot, radish, & ginger juice**, omit the potato and cucumber and add 1 inch peeled and roughly chopped fresh ginger root. This is a good juice if you have a cold or blocked sinuses.

# carrot, chili, & pineapple juice

Makes ¾ **cup**

½ small **chili**
8 oz **pineapple**
8 oz **carrot**
**ice cubes**
juice of ½ **lime**
1 tablespoon chopped
  **cilantro leaves**

**Seed** the chili. Remove the core and peel from the pineapple. Juice the carrots with the chili and pineapple.

**Pour** the juice into a glass over ice. Squeeze over the lime juice, stir in the chopped cilantro, and serve immediately.

**For tomato, celery, & ginger juice**, trim 3 celery sticks and roughly chop 1 inch piece each of fresh ginger root and fresh horseradish. Juice the celery, ginger, and horseradish with 10 oz tomatoes, 6 oz carrot, and a garlic clove. Serve over ice, decorated with celery slivers, if desired.

# carrot, endive, & celery juice

Makes ¾ **cup**

6 oz **carrot**
3 **celery sticks**
4 oz **Belgian endive**
2–3 **ice cubes**
**lemon slices**, to serve
chopped **parsley**, to serve
    (optional)

**Scrub** the carrots. Trim the celery and cut it into 2 inch lengths. Juice the endive with the carrot and the celery.

**Transfer** the juice to a food processor or blender, add a couple of ice cubes, and process briefly.

**Pour** the juice into a glass, decorate with slices of lemon and some chopped parsley, if desired, and serve immediately.

**For carrot & cabbage juice**, juice 8 oz each of carrot and cabbage and serve over ice. This quick juice soothes upset stomachs.

# parsnip, green pepper, & watercress juice

Makes ¾ **cup**

6 oz **green bell pepper**
2½ cups **watercress**
6 oz **cucumber**
6 oz **parsnip**
**ice cubes**
chopped **mint**, to decorate

**Core** and seed the pepper. Juice the watercress and cucumber with the parsnip and pepper.

**Pour** the juice into a tall glass over ice, decorate with a sprinkling of mint, and serve immediately.

**For watercress & pear juice**, juice 1 cup watercress with 3 ripe pears. This simple juice is highly nutritious.

# seven vegetable juice

Makes ¾ **cup**

2 oz **green bell pepper**
1 large **celery stick**
3 oz **carrot**
½ cup **spinach**
¼ **onion**
½ **cucumber**
2 oz **tomatoes**, plus extra
   to serve (optional)
**sea salt and pepper**

**Core** and seed the pepper. Trim the celery and cut it into 2 inch lengths. Juice the carrot, spinach, onion, cucumber, and tomato with the pepper and celery, taking care that the spinach leaves do not clog the machine.

**Pour** the juice into a glass and season with sea salt and black pepper. Decorate with tomato quarters, if desired, and serve immediately.

**For yellow pepper, spinach, & apple juice**, core and seed 4 oz yellow bell pepper and juice the flesh with 2½ cups spinach and 8 oz apple.

# cabbage, apple, & cinnamon juice

Makes ¾ **cup**

7 oz **green cabbage**
2 oz **apple**
2–3 **ice cubes**
**ground cinnamon**, plus extra
   to decorate

**Separate** the cabbage into leaves and cut the apple into pieces. Juice the cabbage with the apple.

**Transfer** the juice to a food processor or blender, add a couple of ice cubes and a sprinkling of cinnamon, and process briefly.

**Pour** the juice into a glass, decorate with a sprinkling of cinnamon, and serve immediately.

**For red cabbage, grape, & orange juice**, juice 4 oz red cabbage with half an orange and a handful of seedless red grapes to make a colorful and only slightly sweet drink.

# cabbage & pear juice

Makes ¾ **cup**

4 oz **cabbage**
1 large **celery stick**
½ cup **watercress**
8 oz **pear**
**ice cubes** (optional)
1 **celery stick**, to serve
   (optional)

**Chop** the cabbage roughly. Trim the celery and cut it into 2 inch lengths. Juice the watercress with the pears, cabbage, and celery.

**Pour** the juice into a tall glass over ice, if using, and serve immediately with a short celery stick, if desired.

**For fennel, celery, & grapefruit juice**, juice 4 oz each of celery and fennel with half a grapefruit. Serve with ice.

# spinach, celery, & cucumber juice

Makes ¾ **cup**

2 oz **green bell pepper**
1 large **celery stick**
½ cup **spinach**
½ **cucumber**
4 oz **tomatoes**, plus extra
    to serve (optional)
**salt and pepper**
**ice cubes** (optional)

**Core** and seed the pepper. Trim the celery and cut it into
2 inch lengths. Juice the spinach, cucumber, and tomatoes
with the pepper and celery. Season the juice to taste with
salt and pepper.

**Pour** the juice into a glass over ice, if using, decorate with
tomato quarters, if desired, and serve immediately.

**For kale & spirulina juice**, juice 1 oz kale with 4 oz
wheatgrass. Stir in 1 teaspoon spirulina before serving.
This unusual-tasting juice offers excellent health benefits.

# lettuce, grape, & ginger juice

Makes ¾ **cup**

1 inch piece **fresh ginger
    root**, chopped
1 cup seedless **green grapes,**
    plus extra to decorate
    (optional)
7 oz **lettuce**
**ice cubes** (optional)

**Peel** and roughly chop the ginger. Juice the grapes and
lettuce with the ginger, alternating the ingredients so that
the lettuce leaves do not clog the machine.

**Pour** the juice into a glass, decorate with a few grapes, if
desired, and serve immediately. Alternatively, for a creamier
drink, transfer the juice to a food processor or blender, add
a couple of ice cubes, and process briefly.

**For lettuce & apple juice**, juice 6 oz romaine lettuce with
1 large apple, making sure that the lettuce leaves do not
clog the machine.

# fennel & camomile juice

Makes ¾ **cup**

1 **lemon**, plus extra to serve
   (optional)
5 oz **fennel**
½ cup chilled **camomile tea**
**ice cubes**

**Peel** the lemon and juice it with the fennel. Mix the juice with the camomile tea.

**Pour** the juice into a glass over ice and serve with slices of lemon, if desired.

**For fennel & lettuce juice**, juice 4 oz fennel and 6 oz lettuce with half a lemon. Serve with ice and a slice of lemon.

# lettuce & kiwifruit juice

Makes ¾ **cup**

1 **kiwifruit**, plus extra to serve
  (optional)
7 oz **lettuce**
**ice cubes** (optional)

**Peel** the kiwifruit and roughly chop the flesh. Separate
the lettuce into leaves. Juice the kiwifruit and lettuce,
alternating the ingredients so that the lettuce leaves do
not clog the machine.

**Pour** the juice into a glass over ice, if using, decorate with
slices of kiwifruit, if desired, and serve immediately.

**For lettuce & camomile juice**, juice half a lemon with
7 oz lettuce. Mix the juice with ½ cup chilled camomile tea
and serve with a couple of ice cubes and a slice of lemon.

# red onion & beet juice

Makes ¾ **cup**

2½ cups **watercress**
4 oz **red onion**
1 **garlic clove**
8 oz **carrot**
4 oz **beet**, plus leaves to serve
   (optional)

**Juice** the watercress, onion, and garlic with the carrot and beet.

**Pour** the juice into a glass, decorate with beet leaves, if desired, and serve immediately.

**For carrot & beet juice**, peel and roughly chop 1 inch cube fresh ginger root and juice the ginger with 10 large carrots and 4 large beets. Serve over ice.

# jerusalem artichoke, celery, & celeriac juice

Makes ¾ **cup**

4 oz **celeriac**
4 oz **Jerusalem artichokes**
2–3 **celery sticks**
small bunch of **mint**
2–3 **ice cubes**

**Peel** the celeriac and chop the flesh into sticks. Juice with the Jerusalem artichokes, celery, and the mint, alternating the mint leaves with the other ingredients to make sure that the leaves do not clog the machine.

**Transfer** the juice to a food processor or blender, add a couple of ice cubes, and process briefly.

**Pour** the juice into a glass and serve immediately.

**For Jerusalem artichoke & carrot juice**, juice 4 oz each of artichokes, carrots, lettuce, Brussels sprouts, and green beans with half a lemon.

# healthy
# smoothies

# cucumber, lemon, & mint smoothie

Makes 1¼ **cups**

1½ **cucumbers**, plus extra
  to serve
½ **lemon**
3–4 fresh **mint leaves**
2–3 **ice cubes**

**Peel** and roughly chop the cucumber. Squeeze the lemon.

**Put** the cucumber and lemon into a food processor or blender with the mint leaves and ice cubes and process briefly.

**Pour** the smoothie into a tall glass, decorate with a strip of cucumber, if desired, and serve immediately.

**For grapefruit & cucumber crush**, chop 1 cucumber and blend it with ⅔ cup grapefruit juice and a handful of ice cubes. Process the ingredients to make an ice-cold slushy drink.

# cucumber lassi

Makes 1¾ **cups**

1 **cucumber**
⅔ cup live **plain yogurt**
6 tablespoons ice-cold
   **still water**
handful of **mint**
½ teaspoon **ground cumin**
squeeze of **lemon juice**

**Peel** and roughly chop the cucumber. Place in a food processor or blender and add the yogurt and ice water.

**Pull** the mint leaves off their stalks, reserving a few for decoration. Chop the remainder roughly and put them into the food processor. Add the cumin and lemon juice and process briefly.

**Pour** the smoothie into a tall glass, decorate with mint leaves, if desired, and serve immediately.

**For mango lassi**, cut the flesh of a mango into cubes and add it to a food processor or blender with ⅔ cup live plain yogurt and the same amount of ice-cold still water, 1 tablespoon rose water, and ¼ teaspoon ground cardamom. Process briefly and serve.

# cranberry & yogurt smoothie

Makes 1¼ **cups**

1 cup **cranberries**
3 tablespoons **Greek** or
  **whole milk yogurt**
6 tablespoons **soy milk**
2–3 **ice cubes**
**artificial sweetener**, to taste

**Put** the cranberries in a food processor or blender, add the yogurt, soy milk, and ice cubes and process.

**Taste** and add artificial sweetener if required. Process once again.

**Pour** the smoothie into a large glass and serve immediately.

**For raspberry shake**, put ⅔ cup soy milk and 1 cup frozen raspberries in a food processor or blender and process until smooth.

# cranberry & apple smoothie

Makes ¾ **cup**

8 oz **apple**
1 cup frozen **cranberries**
6 tablespoons live **plain yogurt**
1 tablespoon **honey**
**ice cubes** (optional)

**Juice** the apples.

**Transfer** the juice to a food processor or blender, add the cranberries, yogurt, and honey and process briefly.

**Pour** the smoothie into a glass over ice, if using, and serve immediately.

**For grapeberry smoothie**, blend together ¾ cup blackberries, 1¼ cups purple grape juice, and 3 tablespoons live plain yogurt.

# mandarin & litchi frappé

Makes ⅔ **cup**

3½ oz **mandarin oranges**,
  canned in natural juice
2 oz **litchis**, canned in natural
  juice
**ice cubes**

**Put** the oranges and litchis and the juices from the cans into a food processor or blender, add the ice cubes, and process briefly.

**Pour** the frappé into a glass and serve immediately.

**For ruby smoothie**, put the juice of 2 oranges and 1 apple in a food processor or blender with 1 cup each raspberries and strawberries. Add ⅔ cup live plain yogurt and process briefly.

# orange super-smoothie

Makes ¾ **cup**

1 large **carrot**
1 **orange**
1 **banana**
1 fresh or dried **apricot**
2–3 **ice cubes**

**Juice** the carrot and orange together.

**Transfer** the juice to a food processor or blender, add the banana, apricot, and a couple of ice cubes, and blend briefly.

**Pour** the smoothie into a glass and serve immediately.

**For orange & banana smoothie**, which makes a great breakfast or lunch, place 1 banana, ⅔ cup fresh orange juice, and ¼ cup sunflower seeds in a food processor or blender and blend together.

# orange, mango, & strawberry smoothie

Makes 1¾ **cups**

¾ cup **strawberries**
1 small ripe **mango**
1¼ cups **orange juice**
**orange slices**, to decorate
(optional)

**Hull** the strawberries, put them in a freezer container, and freeze for 2 hours or overnight.

**Peel** the mango, remove the pit, roughly chop the flesh, and put it in a food processor or blender with the strawberries and orange juice and process until thick.

**Pour** the smoothie into a tall glass, decorate with slices of orange, if desired, and serve immediately.

**For orange & banana smoothie**, blend a ripe banana with the strawberries and orange juice. Serve decorated with orange slices, if desired.

# banana & peanut butter smoothie

Makes 1¾ **cups**

1 ripe **banana**
1¼ cups **lowfat milk**
1 tablespoon smooth **peanut butter** or 2 teaspoons **tahini paste**

**Peel** and slice the banana, put it in a freezer container, and freeze for at least 2 hours or overnight.

**Put** the banana, milk, and peanut butter or tahini paste in a food processor or blender and process until smooth.

**Pour** the smoothie into a tall glass and serve immediately.

**For banana almond smoothie**, put 2 frozen bananas, 2 cups soy milk, ⅓ cup ground almonds, and a pinch of cinnamon into a food processor or blender and process briefly.

# banana, orange, & mango smoothie

Makes **2 cups**

1 ripe **banana**
1 ripe **mango**
¾ cup **orange juice**
¾ cup **lowfat milk**
3 tablespoons **fromage frais**
  or **plain yogurt**
**ice cubes** (optional)

**Peel** and slice the banana. Peel the mango, remove the pit, and cut the flesh into even-size pieces.

**Put** the banana and mango in a food processor or blender, add the orange juice, milk, and fromage frais or yogurt, and process until smooth.

**Pour** the smoothie into 2 glasses over ice, if using, and serve immediately.

**For banana & avocado smoothie**, process 1 small ripe banana with 1 small ripe avocado and 1 cup skim milk.

# banana & fig smoothie

Makes ¾ **cup**

1 inch piece **fresh ginger root**
4 oz **fig**, plus extra to serve
   (optional)
1 **orange**
8 oz **carrot**
1 **banana**
**ice cubes**

**Peel** and roughly chop the ginger. Juice the fig and orange
with the carrot and ginger.

**Transfer** the juice to a food processor or blender, add the
banana and some ice cubes, and process until smooth.

**Pour** the drink into a glass, add more ice cubes, decorate
with sliced figs, if desired, and serve immediately.

**For banana & papaya smoothie**, put the flesh of a
papaya in a food processor or blender with a banana, the
juice of 1 orange, 1¼ cups apple juice, and some ice.
Process until smooth.

146

# prune, apple, & cinnamon smoothie

Makes 1¾ **cups**

⅓ cup ready-to-eat **prunes**
pinch of **ground cinnamon**,
    plus extra to serve
1½ cups **apple juice**
3 tablespoons **Greek** or
    **whole milk yogurt**
**ice cubes**

**Roughly** chop the prunes. Put the prunes and cinnamon in
a large bowl, pour over the apple juice, cover, and allow to
stand overnight.

**Put** the prunes, apple juice, and yogurt in a food processor
or blender and process until smooth.

**Pour** the smoothie into a large glass over ice cubes,
sprinkle with extra cinnamon, and drink immediately.

**For apple & avocado smoothie**, process the flesh of
a small, ripe avocado with ½ cup apple juice.

# apple, banana, & wheatgerm smoothie

Makes **4 cups**

2 tablespoons **wheatgerm**
1 tablespoon **sesame seeds**
2 **bananas**
3 oz **pineapple**
2 cups **apple juice**
1¼ cups **live plain yogurt**

**Spread** the wheatgerm and sesame seeds over a baking sheet and toast gently under a preheated broiler, stirring a couple of times until the sesame seeds have begun to turn a golden brown. Remove from the broiler and allow to cool.

**Peel** and slice the bananas. Remove the skin and core from the pineapple and chop the flesh. Put the banana and pineapple in a food processor or blender and process to a rough puree.

**Add** the apple juice and blend again to make a smooth juice. Add the yogurt and the cooled wheatgerm and sesame seeds. Blend again.

**Pour** the smoothie into a pitcher and serve immediately in glasses.

**For apple & oat smoothie**, process an apple and a banana with ⅔ cup live plain yogurt, ¾ cup skim milk, a few drops of vanilla extract, 2 teaspoons honey, and 2 tablespoons granola in a food processor or blender.

# summer berry smoothie

Makes 1¾ **cups**

1 cup frozen **mixed summer
  berries**, plus extra to serve
  (optional)
1¼ cups **vanilla-flavored
  soy milk**
1 teaspoon **honey** (optional)

**Put** the berries, soy milk, and honey, if using, in a food
processor or blender and process until thick.

**Pour** the smoothie into 2 short glasses, decorate with
berries, if desired, and serve immediately.

**For blueberry & grape smoothie**, blend together 1 cup
frozen blueberries, 1¼ cups red grapes, and 3 tablespoons
fromage frais or plain yogurt.

# blueberry & mint smoothie

Makes **1 cup**

1 cup frozen **blueberries**
⅔ cup **soy milk**
small bunch of **mint**

**Put** the blueberries in a food processor or blender and pour in the soy milk. Pull the mint leaves off their stalks, reserving one or two sprigs for decoration, and add the remainder to the blender. Process briefly.

**Pour** the smoothie into a glass, decorate with the reserved mint sprigs, and serve immediately.

**For blueberry & apple smoothie**, process 8 oz apples with 1 cup blueberries in a food processor or blender until smooth.

# beet & berry smoothie

Makes **1 cup**

2 oz **beet**
1 cup **blueberries**, plus extra
   to serve (optional)
1 cup **raspberries**
2–3 **ice cubes**

**Juice** the beet.

**Pour** the beet juice into a food processor or blender, add
the blueberries, raspberries, and ice cubes and process
until smooth.

**Pour** the mixture into a glass, decorate with blueberries, if
desired, and serve immediately.

**For blueberry & grapefruit smoothie**, juice 4 oz grapefruit
with 8 oz apples. Transfer the juice to a food processor or
blender with 1 cup blueberries and 1 inch piece fresh
ginger root and process until smooth.

# raspberry, kiwifruit, & grapefruit smoothie

Makes ¾ **cup**

5 oz **grapefruit**
6 oz **pineapple**
1 **kiwifruit**
½ cup frozen **raspberries**, plus
   extra to serve (optional)
½ cup frozen **cranberries**

**Peel** and segment the grapefruit. Remove the skin and core from the pineapple. Juice the kiwifruit with the grapefruit and pineapple.

**Transfer** the juice to a food processor or blender, add the frozen berries, and process until smooth.

**Pour** the smoothie into a glass, decorate with raspberries, if desired, and serve with a straw.

**For strawberry & pineapple smoothie**, process 1 cup frozen strawberries with ⅔ cup pineapple juice and ⅔ cup strawberry yogurt.

# strawberry lassi

Makes **6 cups**

3 cups **strawberries**
3 cups **ice-cold water**
1¼ cups **low-fat live plain yogurt**
2 tablespoons **superfine sugar**
few drops of **rose water**
coarsely ground **black pepper**, to serve

**Hull** and roughly chop the strawberries. Put them in a food processor or blender with half the water and process until smooth.

**Add** the yogurt, sugar, rose water, and the remaining water and process again until smooth and frothy.

**Pour** the smoothie into chilled glasses, sprinkle with black pepper, and serve immediately.

**For banana lassi**, process 2 small ripe bananas with 1¼ cups live plain yogurt, ½ cup ice-cold water, and a pinch of ground cardamom in a food processor or blender.

# mango, pineapple, & lime smoothie

Makes 1¾ **cups**

1 ripe **mango**
1¼ cups **pineapple juice**
zest and juice of ½ **lime**
**lime wedges**, to serve
   (optional)

**Peel** the mango, remove the pit, roughly chop the flesh, and put it in a freezer container. Freeze for at least 2 hours or overnight.

**Put** the frozen mango in a food processor or blender, add the pineapple juice and lime zest and juice, and process until thick.

**Pour** the smoothie into 2 short glasses, decorate with lime wedges, if desired, and serve immediately.

**For apricot & pineapple smoothie**, soak ⅓ cup dried apricots overnight in 1½ cups pineapple juice. Process the mixture in a food processor or blender with some ice until smooth.

# mango & mint sherbet

Makes **6 cups**

3 ripe **mangoes**
4 tablespoons **lemon juice**
1 tablespoon **superfine sugar**
12 **mint leaves**, finely
  chopped
3¾ cups ice-cold **water**
**ice cubes**

**Peel** and pit the mangoes and roughly chop the flesh. Put it into a food processor or blender with the lemon juice, sugar, mint leaves, and water and process until smooth.

**Pour** the smoothie into tall glasses over ice and serve immediately.

**For mango & black currant smoothie**, process the flesh of 3 mangoes with ½ cup apple juice and 1¾ cups black currants.

# mango, coconut, & lime lassi

Makes **2½ cups**

1 large ripe **mango**
juice of 1 **orange**
juice of 1 **lime**
1 tablespoon **honey**
1¼ cups **plain yogurt**
4 tablespoons **coconut milk**
**orange slices**, to decorate
   (optional)
**ice cubes** (optional)

**Peel** the mango, remove the pit, and dice the flesh. Put the mango in a food processor or blender with the orange and lime juices, honey, yogurt, and coconut milk. Process until smooth.

**Transfer** the mixture to a pitcher then pour into tall glasses over ice, if using, decorate with slices of orange, if desired, and serve immediately.

**For pineapple & coconut smoothie**, process 4 oz pineapple flesh with 6 tablespoons coconut milk and 6 tablespoons soy milk. Serve sprinkled with toasted coconut.

# tropical fruit smoothie

Makes 2½ **cups**

1 large **banana**
1 large ripe **mango**
⅔ cup **plain yogurt**
1¼ cups **pineapple juice**
**pineapple chunks**, to serve
    (optional)

**Peel** and slice the banana, then put it in a freezer-proof container and freeze for at least 2 hours or overnight.

**Peel** the mango, remove the pit, and roughly chop the flesh. Place the flesh in a food processor or blender with the frozen banana, yogurt, and pineapple juice and process until smooth.

**Pour** the mixture into tall glasses, decorate with pineapple chunks, if desired, and serve immediately.

**For kiwifruit, melon, & passion fruit smoothie**, freeze 2 cups watermelon flesh, then blend it with 2 kiwifruit and add ¾ cup passion fruit juice.

# peach & tofu smoothie

Makes 1¼ **cups**

1 oz **peach**
½ cup **tofu**
⅓ cup **vanilla ice cream**
6 tablespoons **still water**
few drops of natural **almond
   extract**
**ice cubes** (optional)

**Halve** the peach, remove the skin and pit, and roughly chop the peach flesh.

**Put** the peach in a food processor or blender and add the tofu and ice cream. Pour in the water, add a little almond extract, and process until smooth.

**Pour** the mixture into 2 short glasses over ice, if using, and serve immediately.

**For rhubarb smoothie**, blend ½ cup stewed rhubarb with ½ cup live plain yogurt, and 2 drops of vanilla extract. Sweeten to taste with honey.

# peach & orange smoothie

Makes ¾ **cup**

7 oz **peaches, canned in
  natural juice**
5 tablespoons **peach- or
  apricot-flavored yogurt,**
  plus extra to serve
6 tablespoons **orange juice**
1 teaspoon **honey** (optional)
**ice cubes** (optional)

**Drain** the peaches and discard the juice.

**Put** the peaches into a food processor or blender with
the yogurt, orange juice, and honey, if using, and process
until smooth.

**Pour** the smoothie into a glass over ice, if using, top with
a swirl of any remaining yogurt, and serve immediately.

**For peach, pear, & raspberry smoothie**, blend 1 peach
and 1 pear and with 1 cup raspberries. Add ⅔ cup peach
juice to make a tangy drink.

# marbled peach milkshake

Makes **3¾ cups**

2½ cups **raspberries**
4 teaspoons **honey**
2 large juicy **peaches**
1 teaspoon **vanilla bean
  paste** or a few drops
  **vanilla extract**
½ cup **light cream**
⅔ cup **orange juice**

**Put** the raspberries in a food processor or blender and process to make a smooth puree. Press this through a nonmetallic strainer to remove the seeds, and stir in half the honey. Check the sweetness, adding a little more honey if necessary.

**Halve** the peaches, remove the pits, and coarsely chop the flesh. Blend the peaches to a puree with the vanilla bean paste or extract and cream. Blend in the orange juice and any remaining honey.

**Spoon** a layer of the peach puree to a depth of about ¾ inch in 2 large glasses. Add a layer of raspberry puree and repeat the layering. Lightly marble the colors together with a knife and serve.

**For vanilla yogurt smoothie**, blend ¾ cup live plain yogurt with 1 teaspoon vanilla bean paste, 2 tablespoons honey, and 1¼ cups apple juice.

# rhubarb & custard smoothie

Makes **1¾ cups**

5 oz **canned rhubarb**
⅔ cup **ready-made custard**
6 tablespoons ice-cold **lowfat milk**
1 teaspoon **confectioners' sugar** (optional)
**ice cubes** (optional)

**Drain** the rhubarb and discard the juice.

**Put** the rhubarb in a food processor with the custard, milk, and confectioners' sugar, if using, and process until smooth.

**Pour** the smoothie into a large glass over ice, if using, and serve immediately.

**For choco-cherry shake**, blend ½ cup pitted cherries with 6 tablespoons soy milk and 1 oz melted semisweet chocolate. Serve with ice.

# dried fruit & apple smoothie

Makes 1¾ **cups**

¾ cup **dried fruit salad**
about 1¾ cups **apple juice**
¾ cup **Greek** or **whole milk
    yogurt**
**ice cubes** (optional)

**Roughly** chop the dried fruit salad and place it in a large
bowl. Pour over the apple juice, cover the bowl, and allow to
stand overnight.

**Put** the dried fruit salad and apple juice in a food processor
or blender, add the yogurt, and process until smooth, adding
a little more apple juice if necessary.

**Pour** the smoothie into 2 glasses, add a couple of ice
cubes, if using, and serve immediately.

**For apricot smoothie**, process 7 oz canned apricots in
natural juice with ⅔ cup apricot yogurt, and ⅔ cup ice-
cold lowfat milk.

# watermelon cooler

**Makes 1¼ cups**

4 oz **watermelon**
⅔ cup **strawberries**
6 tablespoons **still water**
small handful of **mint or
   tarragon leaves**, plus extra
   to serve (optional)

**Skin** and seed the melon and chop the flesh into cubes.
Hull the strawberries. Freeze the melon and strawberries
until solid.

**Put** the frozen melon and strawberries in a food processor
or blender, add the water and the mint or tarragon, and
process until smooth.

**Pour** the mixture into 2 short glasses, decorate with mint or
tarragon leaves, if desired, and serve immediately.

**For melon & almond smoothie**, process 4 oz frozen galia
melon flesh with 6 tablespoons almond milk.

# red pepper & tomato smoothie

Makes ¾ **cup**

2 oz **red bell pepper**
2 oz **cucumber**
2 **scallions**
6 tablespoons **tomato juice**
splash of **lemon juice**
splash of **hot pepper sauce**
splash of **Worcestershire**
   **sauce**
**salt and pepper**

**Core** and seed the red pepper and roughly chop the flesh.
Peel the cucumber and roughly chop the flesh. Roughly
chop the scallions, reserving a few shreds for a garnish.

**Pour** the tomato juice into a food processor or blender, add
the pepper, cucumber, and scallion and process briefly.
Taste, then season to taste with lemon juice, hot pepper
sauce, Worcestershire sauce, and salt and pepper.

**Pour** the smoothie into a glass, garnish with the remaining
scallion, and serve immediately.

**For guacamole smoothie**, add 2 scallions, half a
chopped chili, half a ripe avocado, and 6 tablespoons
tomato juice to a food processor or blender and process
until smooth. Serve with ice and some chopped cilantro.

# juices &
# smoothies
# for kids

# mango & melon juice

Makes 1¾ **cups**

1 ripe **mango**
½ **galia melon**
¾ cup **orange juice**
**ice cubes**

**Peel** the mango, remove the pit, and roughly chop the flesh.
Peel and seed the melon and roughly chop the flesh.

**Put** the mango and melon in a food processor or blender,
add the orange juice and a couple of ice cubes, and
process until smooth.

**Pour** the juice into 2 short glasses and serve immediately.

**For grape & melon juice**, juice 5 oz galia melon flesh with
1 cup seedless green grapes. Dilute with ⅔ cup water.

# mango, orange, & cranberry juice

Makes ¾ **cup**

1 **mango**
1 **orange**
1 cup **cranberries**
6 tablespoons **still water**
1 teaspoon **honey**
**ice cubes** (optional)

**Peel** the mango and remove the pit. Peel the orange and divide the flesh into segments. Juice the cranberries with the mango and orange.

**Pour** the juice into a glass and stir in the water and honey. Add a couple of ice cubes, if using, and serve immediately.

**For kiwifruit, orange, & strawberry juice**, juice 2 oranges and 1 kiwifruit with 1⅓ cups strawberries.

# melon, carrot, & ginger juice

Makes ¾ **cup**

8 oz **cantaloupe melon**
1 **lime**
½ inch piece **fresh ginger root**
4 oz **carrot**
**ice cubes**, to serve (optional)

**Peel** and seed the melon and cut the flesh into cubes. Peel the lime. Peel and roughly chop the ginger. Juice the carrot with the melon, lime, and ginger.

**Pour** the juice into a glass over ice, if using, and serve immediately.

**For carrot, orange, & apple juice**, juice 2 carrots with 1 orange and 1 apple.

# pear & pineapple juice

**Makes ¾ cup**

7 oz **fresh pineapple** or
   **canned pineapple in**
   **its own juices**
½ **lemon**
2 **pears**
**ice cubes**

**Peel** and core the fresh pineapple and cut the flesh into
pieces. If using canned pineapple, drain and discard the
juice. Juice the lemon with the pineapple and pears.

**Pour** the juice into a glass over ice and serve immediately.

**For pear & kiwifruit juice**, replace both the lemon and
pineapple with 3 kiwifruit. This is an excellent juice for
all-round good health.

# apple, pineapple, & melon juice

Makes ¾ **cup**

½ **galia melon**
¼ **pineapple**
3 **green apples**
**ice cubes** (optional)

**Peel** and seed the melon. Remove the skin and hard core from the pineapple. Chop all the fruit into even-size pieces and juice.

**Pour** the juice into a glass over ice, if using, and serve immediately.

**For plum & apple juice**, remove the pits from 5 ripe plums, then juice them with 3 red apples. Serve this delicious juice over ice.

# orange, apple, & pear juice

Makes ¾ **cup**

2 **oranges**
1 **red apple**
1 **pear**
**ice cubes** (optional)
1 teaspoon **honey** (optional)

**Peel** the oranges and divide the flesh into segments. Chop the apple and pear into even-size pieces. Juice all the fruit.

**Pour** the juice into a glass over ice, if using, stir in the honey, if using, and serve immediately.

**For apple & pear slush**, roughly chop 2 pears and 2 apples, then process the juice in a food processor or blender with some ice.

# apple, peach, & strawberry popsicles

Makes 1¼ **cups**

2 **peaches**
1¼ cups **still water**
1 **red apple**
¾ cup **strawberries**

**Halve** the peaches, remove the pits, roughly chop the flesh and juice.

**Add** one-third of the water and spoon the mixture into 3–4 popsicle molds. Freeze until just set.

**Roughly** chop the apple and juice. Add one-third of the water and pour over the frozen peach mixture. Freeze until just set.

**Hull** the strawberries, then juice them. Add the remainder of the water, pour over the frozen apple mixture, and freeze until set.

**For orange & strawberry juice**, hull 1⅓ cups strawberries and juice them with 2 oranges.

198

# strawberry, red currant, & orange juice

Makes **1 cup**

⅔ cup **strawberries**
¾ cup **red currants**, plus extra
  to serve (optional)
½ **orange**
½ cup **still water**
½ teaspoon **honey** (optional)
**ice cubes**

**Hull** the strawberries. Remove the stalks from the red currants and peel and segment the orange. Juice the fruit, add the water, and stir in the honey, if using.

**Pour** the juice into a glass, add some ice cubes, and decorate with extra red currants, if desired. To make this juice into popsicles, pour into popsicle molds after stirring in the honey and freeze.

**For kiwifruit & orange juice**, roughly chop 3 kiwifruit and juice with 2 large oranges.

# melon, blackberry, & kiwifruit juice

Makes ¾ **cup**

4 oz **cantaloupe melon**
2 **kiwifruit**
⅔ cup fresh or frozen
   **blackberries**, plus extra
   to serve
6 tablespoons **apple juice**
2–3 **ice cubes**

**Cut** the melon into cubes but do not remove the skin. Cut the kiwifruit into slices. Juice the blackberries with the melon and kiwifruit.

**Transfer** the juice to a food processor or blender, add the apple juice and a couple of ice cubes, and process briefly.

**Pour** the juice into a glass, decorate with a few blackberries, and serve immediately.

**For kiwifruit, melon, & grape juice**, roughly chop 2 kiwifruit and juice with 2⅓ cups honeydew melon flesh and ½ cup seedless green grapes. For a change, freeze the juice in popsicle molds.

# kiwifruit, melon, & passion fruit juice

Makes 1¼ **cups**

about 10 oz **watermelon**
2 **kiwifruit**
¾ cup **passion fruit juice**

**Peel** and seed the melon and cut the flesh into cubes. Put the melon in a freezer container and freeze for at least 2 hours or overnight.

**Peel** and roughly chop the kiwifruit, then put them in a food processor or blender with the melon and passion fruit juice and process until thick.

**Pour** the juice into a large glass and serve immediately.

**For kiwifruit, melon, & pineapple juice**, roughly chop 2 kiwifruit and juice with 2 cups watermelon flesh and ¾ cup pineapple juice.

# strawberry, carrot, & beet juice

Makes 1¼ **cups**

8 oz **carrot**
4 oz **beet**
1 **orange**
¾ cup **strawberries**, plus extra
   to serve (optional)
**ice cubes**

**Juice** the carrot, beet, and orange.

**Hull** the strawberries. Put the carrot, beet, and orange juice
in a food processor or blender, add the strawberries and a
few ice cubes, and process until smooth.

**Pour** the juice into a large glass, decorate with a strawberry,
if desired, and serve immediately.

**For strawberry, melon, & cucumber juice**, hull ⅔ cup
strawberries and juice with ½ cup honeydew melon and
half a cucumber.

# tomato, orange, & celery juice

Makes 1¾ **cups**

2 **oranges**
2 **celery sticks**, plus leafy
   stalks to serve
4 **tomatoes**
2 **carrots**
**ice cubes**

**Peel** the oranges. Trim the celery and cut it into 2 inch lengths. Juice the tomatoes and carrots with the oranges and celery.

**Pour** the juice into 2 tall glasses over ice, decorate with leafy celery stalk stirrers, and serve immediately.

**For celery & apple juice**, trim and cut 3 celery sticks into 2 inch lengths. Juice the celery with 2 apples and ½ cup alfalfa sprouts.

# mango, apple, & cucumber juice

Makes ¾ **cup**

7 oz **apple**
4 oz **cucumber**
4 oz **mango**
**ice cubes**

**Peel** the apple and cucumber. Peel the mango, remove the pit, and roughly chop the flesh. Juice with the apples and cucumber.

**Transfer** the juice to a food processor or blender, add a couple of ice cubes, and blend to make a fruity slush. Serve immediately.

**For papaya, orange, & cucumber juice**, juice 4 oz papaya flesh with the same amount of cucumber and 2 oranges.

# pineapple, parsnip, & carrot smoothie

Makes 1¼ **cups**

8 oz **pineapple**, plus extra
  to serve (optional)
4 oz **parsnip**
4 oz **carrot**
5 tablespoons **soy milk**
**ice cubes**

**Peel** the pineapple, remove the core, and cut the flesh into chunks. Juice the parsnips and carrots with the pineapple.

**Transfer** the juice to a food processor or blender, add the soy milk and some ice cubes, and process until smooth.

**Pour** the mixture into 2 short glasses, decorate with pineapple wedges, if desired, and serve immediately.

**For carrot, orange, & banana smoothie**, juice 5 oz carrot with 1 small orange, then process in a food processor or blender with 1 banana and 6 dried apricots.

# raspberry & blueberry smoothie

Makes ¾ **cup**

2 cups **raspberries**
¾ cup **apple juice**
1¾ cups **blueberries**
4 tablespoons **Greek** or
   **whole milk yogurt**
6 tablespoons **skim milk**
1 tablespoon **honey**, or
   to taste
1 tablespoon **wheatgerm**
   (optional)

**Puree** the raspberries with half the apple juice. Puree
the blueberries with the remaining apple juice.

**Mix** together the yogurt, milk, honey, and wheatgerm,
if using, and add a spoonful of the raspberry puree.

**Pour** the blueberry puree into a tall glass. Carefully pour
over the yogurt mixture, and then pour the raspberry puree
over the surface of the yogurt. Serve chilled.

**For vanilla berry juice**, process 1 cup frozen mixed berries
with 1¼ cups vanilla-flavored soy milk and 1 teaspoon honey.

# mango, apple, & black currant smoothie

Makes 1¾ **cups**

3 **mangoes**
2 tablespoons **mango sorbet**
6 tablespoons **apple juice**
1¾ cups **black currants or blueberries**

**Peel** the mangoes, remove the pits, and roughly chop the flesh. Puree the mangoes with the mango sorbet and half the apple juice. Set aside to chill.

**Puree** the blackcurrants with the rest of the apple juice.

**Spoon** the mango smoothie into 2 short glasses. Place a spoon on the surface of the mango, holding it as flat as you can, and pour on the black currant puree. Drag a teaspoon or skewer down the inside of the glass, to make vertical stripes around the glass.

**For blueberry, apple, & honey smoothie**, add 1¾ cups blueberries to a food processor or blender with 6 tablespoons apple juice, 1¼ cups plain yogurt, and 2 tablespoons honey. Process until blended.

# strawberry, mango, & orange popsicles

Makes 1¾ **cups**

¾ cup **strawberries**
1 small ripe **mango**
1¼ cups **orange juice**

**Hull** the strawberries, then freeze them for 2 hours
or overnight.

**Peel** the mango, remove the pit, and roughly chop the flesh.
Process the mango, frozen strawberries, and orange juice in
a food processor or blender until thick.

**Pour** the mixture into popsicle molds and freeze until set.

**For strawberry, orange, & banana smoothie**, peel 1 small
ripe banana and freeze along with ½ cup strawberries for a
couple of hours. Put the fruit in a food processor or blender
with 1 cup orange juice and process until smooth.

# banana, mango, & orange smoothie

Makes 1¾ **cups**

1 ripe **banana**
1 ripe **mango**
¾ cup **orange juice**
¾ cup **lowfat milk**
3 tablespoons **fromage frais**
   or **plain yogurt**
2–3 **ice cubes**

**Peel** and slice the banana. Peel the mango, remove the pit, and roughly chop the flesh.

**Put** the banana, mango, orange juice, milk, fromage frais or yogurt, and a couple of ice cubes in a food processor or blender and process until smooth.

**Pour** the mixture into 2–3 short glasses and serve immediately.

**For papaya, orange, & banana smoothie**, process the flesh of a papaya with a banana in a food processor or blender, then add the juice of 1 orange and 1¼ cups apple juice.

# kiwifruit, mango, & raspberry smoothie

Makes 1¾ **cups**

3 **kiwifruit**
⅔ cup **lemon- or orange-flavored yogurt**
1 small **mango**
2 tablespoons **orange or apple juice**
1¼ cups **raspberries**
1–2 teaspoons **honey**

**Peel** and roughly chop the kiwifruit, then process in a food processor or blender until smooth. Spoon the puree into 2 tall glasses, and top each with a spoonful of yogurt, spreading the yogurt to the sides of the glasses.

**Peel** the mango, remove the pit, and roughly chop the flesh. Blend the mango to a puree with the orange or apple juice and spoon it into the glasses on top of the kiwifruit puree and yogurt. Top with another layer of yogurt.

**Blend** the raspberries and push them through a strainer over a bowl to extract the seeds. Check their sweetness (you might need to stir in a little honey if they're very sharp) and spoon the raspberry puree into the glasses.

**For mango, apple, & passion fruit smoothie**, juice 3 apples. Process the juice in a food processor or blender with the flesh of a mango and 2 passion fruit.

# peach & orange smoothie

Makes 1¾ **cups**

13 oz can **peaches** in
   natural juice
⅔ cup **peach- or apricot-
   flavored yogurt**, plus
   extra to serve
¾ cup **orange juice**
**honey** (optional)
2–3 **ice cubes** (optional)

**Drain** the peaches, discarding the juice, and put them in
a food processor or blender with the yogurt, orange juice,
honey, if using, and a couple of ice cubes, if desired.
Process until smooth.

**Pour** the mixture into 2 short glasses and top with a swirl
of any remaining yogurt.

**For citrus yogurt smoothie**, put 7 oz canned grapefruit
in natural juice in a food processor or blender with ⅔ cup
lemon-flavored yogurt and ⅔ cup lowfat milk. Process
until smooth.

# peach smoothie

Makes ¾ **cup**

1 large **peach**
⅔ cup **plain yogurt**
3 tablespoons **milk**
**raspberries**, to decorate

**Skin** the peach, remove the pit, and roughly chop the flesh.
Put the peach, yogurt, and milk in a food processor or
blender and process until smooth.

**Pour** the smoothie into a glass, decorate with raspberries,
and serve immediately.

**For pineapple, banana, & strawberry smoothie**, juice
⅔ cup strawberries with 2 cups pineapple. Put the juice in
a food processor or blender, add a banana, and process
until smooth.

# strawberry & soy smoothie

Makes ¾ **cup**

¾ cup fresh or frozen
  **strawberries**
¾ cup **soy milk**
2 **kiwifruit**
**ice cubes** (optional)
¼ cup **slivered almonds**,
  to decorate (optional)

**Hull** the strawberries. Put them into a food processor or
blender with the soy milk and kiwifruit and process briefly.
If you are using fresh rather than frozen strawberries add
a few ice cubes, if using, and process until smooth.

**Pour** the mixture into a glass, decorate with slivered
almonds, if desired, and serve immediately.

**For summer berry & honey smoothie**, put 1 cup
frozen mixed berries into a food processor or blender
with 1¼ cups grape juice, 3 tablespoons quark or plain
yogurt, and 1 teaspoon honey. Process until smooth.

# banana & chocolate smoothie

Makes 1¾ **cups**

1 **banana**
2 tablespoons organic **cocoa
   powder**
1¼ cups **lowfat milk**
6 tablespoons **apple juice**
2 large scoops vanilla **ice
   cream**
**cocoa powder or chocolate
   shavings,** to decorate

**Peel** and roughly chop the banana. Place in a food
processor or blender with the cocoa powder, milk, apple
juice, and ice cream and process until smooth.

**Pour** the mixture into 2 tall glasses, dust with cocoa
powder or chocolate shavings, and serve.

**For banana & peanut butter smoothie**, put a banana,
1¼ cups lowfat milk, and a tablespoon of smooth peanut
butter into a food processor or blender and process
until smooth.

# banana & mango smoothie

Makes **2½ cups**

1 large **banana**, plus extra
  to serve (optional)
1 large ripe **mango**
⅔ cup **plain yogurt**
1¼ cups **pineapple juice**

**Peel** and slice the banana, then put it in a freezer container and freeze for at least 2 hours or overnight.

**Peel** the mango, remove the pit, and cut the flesh into cubes.

**Put** the frozen banana, mango, yogurt, and pineapple juice into a food processor or blender, process until smooth.

**Pour** the mixture into 3 glasses, decorate with a slice of banana, if desired, and serve immediately.

**For cinnamon yogurt banana smoothie**, blend a small ripe banana with 1 cup live plain yogurt, a pinch of cinnamon, and honey, to taste.

# index

# acknowledgments

**Executive Editor** Nicky Hill
**Contributing Editor** Sarah Ford
**Editor** Lisa John
**Executive Art Editor** Mark Stevens
**Designer** Geoff Borin
**Photographer** Lis Parsons
**Home Economist** Alice Storey
**Prop Stylist** Liz Hippisley
**Senior Production Controller** Martin Croshaw

**Commissioned photography** © Octopus Publishing Group Limited/Lis Parsons apart from the following: Octopus Publishing Group Limited/Gareth Sambridge 11, 13, 24, 24, 26, 34, 86, 130, 170, 180; /Janine Hosegood 12, 28, 36, 76, 90; /Jeremy Hopley 64; /Karen Thomas 152; /Stephen Conroy 8; /Vanessa Davies 9, 186, 188, 205, 210, 214, 216, 222, 224, 230.